PETER SCULTHORPE

Three Pieces for Piano

Djilile, Callabonna, Simori

FABER *ff* MUSIC

© 1997 by Faber Music Ltd
First published in 1997 by Faber Music Ltd
3 Queen Square London WC1N 3AU
Music processed by Donald Sheppard
Cover design by S & M Tucker
Printed in England by Halstan & Co Ltd
All rights reserved

ISBN 0 571 51726 9

Djilile

(1986/89)
Duration 5½ minutes.
The first performance was given by Stephen Savage in the
Basil Jones Theatre, Brisbane on 12 May 1989

Callabonna

(1963/89)
Duration 4 minutes.
The first performance was given by Linda Kouvaras
in Melba Hall, The University of Melbourne,
on 30 July 1989

Simori

(1995)
Duration 10½ minutes.
The first performance was given by Ian Munro at the
Deal Festival of Music, England, on 29 July 1995

Djilile is recorded by Alex Furman and Callabonna by
Linda Kouvaras on Peter Sculthorpe Piano Music: Move MD 3031(CD).
Djilile is also recorded by Lisa Moore on Stroke: Tall Poppies TP040 (CD),
by Elizabeth Green on Biodiversity, Vol.1: BD01 (CD) and by Geoffrey Tozer
on Landscapes: MB 16 (CD).
Simori is recorded by Ian Munro on Mere Bagatelles Tall Poppies TP080 (CD).

PROGRAMME NOTES

Djilile

Djilile is based upon an adaptation of an Aboriginal melody collected in northern Australia, in the late 1950s, by A P Elkin and Trevor Jones. The title means 'whistling-duck on a billabong'.

I have a special fondness for this melody, having used it in the string work *Port Essington* (1977), and later in the orchestral work *Kakadu* (1988) and in *Dream Tracks* (1992), for clarinet, violin and piano. I made this piano arrangement of it, with additional material, for my own pleasure, and for the pleasure of some of my friends.

Callabonna

The work takes its name from Lake Callabonna, in the north-western desert of South Australia. The painter Russell Drysdale often remarked that my music reminded him of this place.

A short work in three parts, *Callabonna* marks the beginning of my friendship, in the early sixties, with the painter. It is also concerned with my first real knowledge, through him, of the plight of Australia's aboriginal people. Since that time, this has been a continuing concern in my music.

Simori

This work is based upon a sequence of songs belonging to the Simori mountain people of Papua New Guinea. The songs were brought to light by the Dutch ethnomusicologist Jaap Kunst. They are:

I Yu,   a war cry
II Wani,   a song of welcome
III Kamu,   a song to drive away spirits
IV Pota,   a song of mourning
V Yu,   a cry of joy

The work does not set out to sound like Simori music, nor does it seek to depict the highlands of the central-west of Papua New Guinea: it is more an exploration of the musical ideas of the Simori people.

Simori was written for Ian Munro and premiered by him at the Deal Festival of Music, England, on 29 July 1995.

PS

Djilile

PETER SCULTHORPE

*Bring out the melody, but do not force the sound.

4

tempo primo

molto rall.

meno mosso

Sydney, March 1989

*come sopra

Callabonna

PETER SCULTHORPE

Launceston, October 1963

Simori

PETER SCULTHORPE

I Yu

II Wani

12

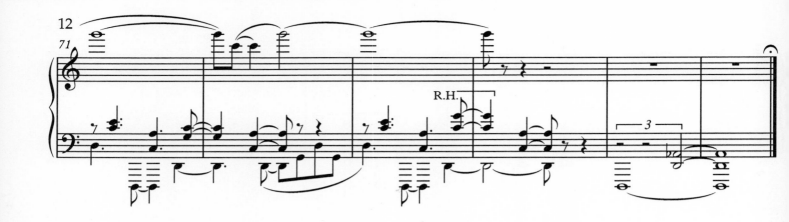

III Kamu

Drammatico (♪. = c.132)

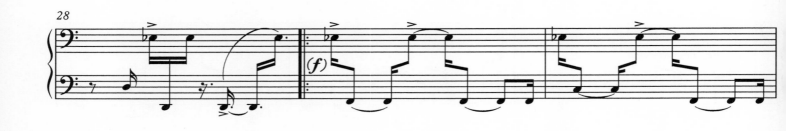

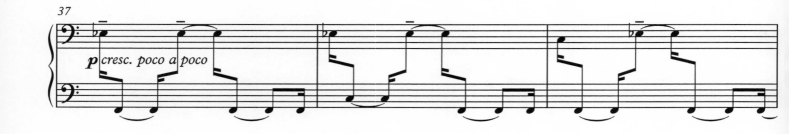

IV Pota

Con tristezza (♩ = c.56)

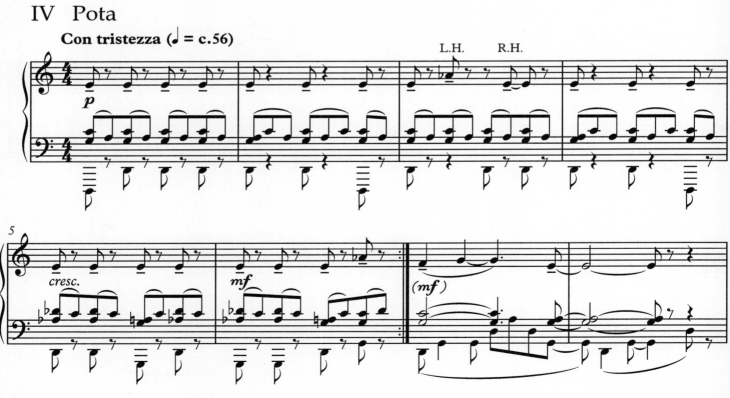

V Yu

Marcato (♩. = c.112)

Sydney, August 1995